Drawing Is Fun

DRAWING
MINIBEASTS

W

FRANKLIN WATTS
LONDON • SYDNEY

First published in 2012 by Franklin Watts

Copyright © 2012 Arcturus Publishing Limited

Franklin Watts
338 Euston Road
London NW1 3BH

Franklin Watts Australia
Level 17/207 Kent Street, Sydney NSW 2000

Produced by Arcturus Publishing Limited,
26/27 Bickels Yard, 151–153 Bermondsey Street, London SE1 3HA

The rights of Rebecca Clunes and Dynamo Limited to be identified as the authors of this work
have been asserted by them in accordance with the Copyright, Designs and Patents Act 1988.

Cartoon illustrations: Dynamo Limited
Text: Rebecca Clunes and Dynamo Limited
Editors: Anna Brett, Kate Overy and Joe Harris
Design: Tokiko Morishima
Cover design: Tokiko Morishima

Picture credits: All photographs supplied by Shutterstock.

A CIP catalogue record for this book is available from the British Library.

Dewey Decimal Classification Number 743.6'57

ISBN 978 1 4451 1022 6

Printed in China

Franklin Watts is a division of Hachette Children's Books, an Hachette UK company.
www.hachette.co.uk

SL001842EN
Supplier 03, Date 0112, Print Run 1429

Contents

Scorpion

This scorpion's tail has a sting at the end.

She curls her tail up over her back.

She has big claws for grabbing hold of her food.

She has eight legs.

FUN FACTS ● FUN FACTS ● FUN FACTS ● FUN FACTS ● FUN FACTS

Mother scorpions look after their babies. They climb on her back and hitch a ride!

1. This shape makes the body and the tail.

2. Add snapping claws at the front.

3. Don't forget the legs on either side of the body.

4. Colour your scorpion, but make sure that you don't get stung by that tail!

Praying mantis

This praying mantis is green so he can hide in the leaves.

He has good eyesight.

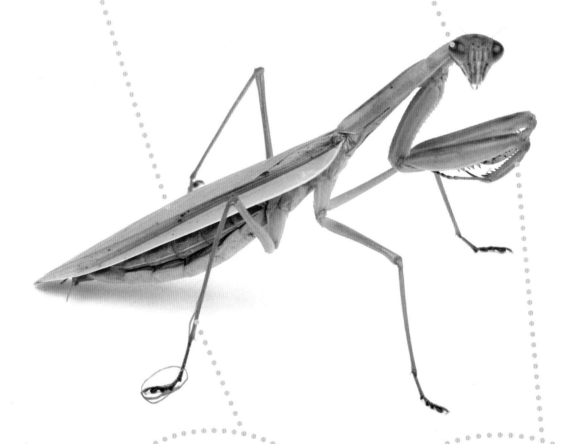

He has four thin back legs for walking.

His front legs can shoot out very fast to grab his food.

FUN FACTS ● FUN FACTS ● FUN FACTS ● FUN FACTS ● FUN FACTS

Praying mantises are very fussy eaters. They will not eat the wings or legs of any insects that they catch.

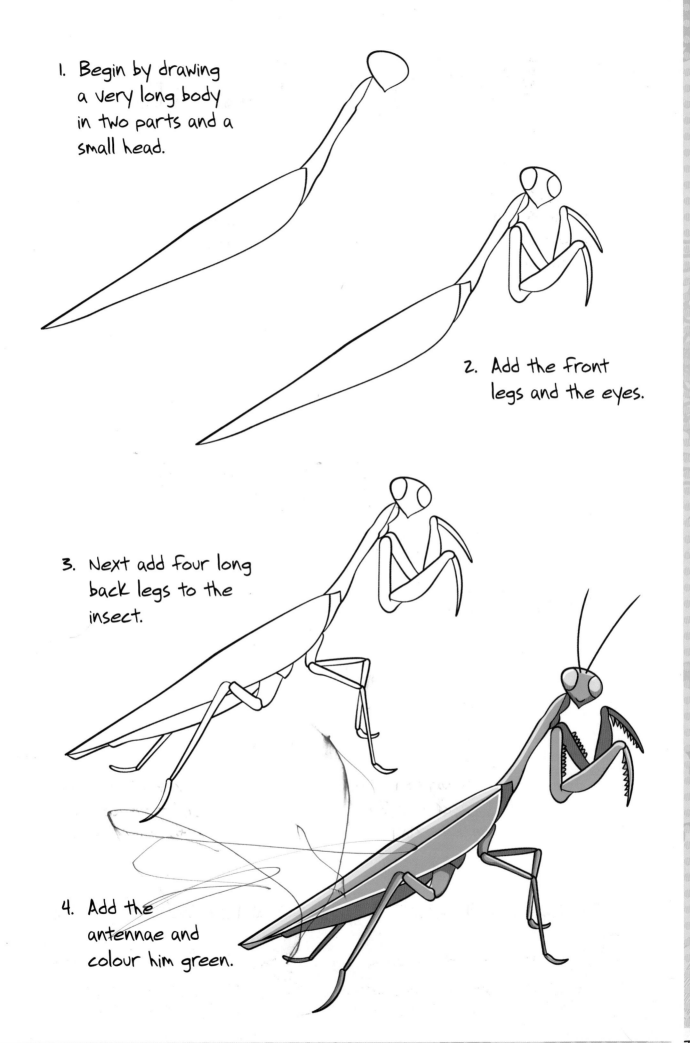

1. Begin by drawing a very long body in two parts and a small head.

2. Add the front legs and the eyes.

3. Next add four long back legs to the insect.

4. Add the antennae and colour him green.

Fly

This fly has a hairy body.

She has two wings and is very good at flying.

Her big eyes allow her to see all around her.

She tastes her food through her feet.

FUN FACTS ● FUN FACTS ● FUN FACTS ● FUN FACTS ● FUN FACTS

Flies eat rotting meat and fruit.

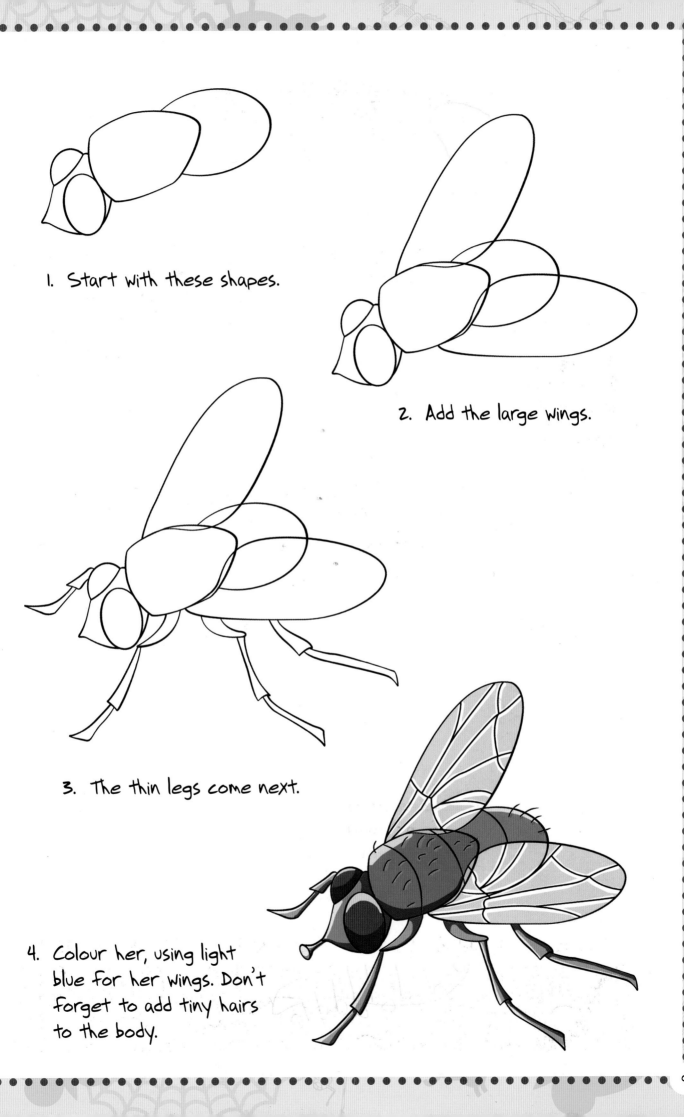

1. Start with these shapes.

2. Add the large wings.

3. The thin legs come next.

4. Colour her, using light
   blue for her wings. Don't
   forget to add tiny hairs
   to the body.

Caterpillar

This caterpillar eats leaves. He grows very fast.

When he gets too big for his old skin, he will wriggle out of it. There is a new, bigger skin underneath.

He can hang from a silk thread that comes out of his mouth.

He has a long, round body and lots of legs.

FUN FACTS ● FUN FACTS ● FUN FACTS ● FUN FACTS ● FUN FACTS

Caterpillars hatch out of eggs. Later they will turn into butterflies or moths.

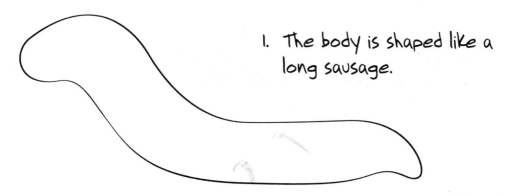

1. The body is shaped like a long sausage.

2. Draw lots of little legs along the bottom of the body.

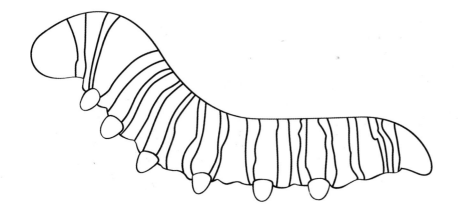

3. Add plenty of stripes to make him stand out.

4. Lots of bright colours and long antennae finish off this happy caterpillar.

Snail

This snail's eyes are at the top of her two biggest feelers.

She can tuck her body inside her shell if she is in danger.

The shorter feelers are used for smelling.

She has no legs and moves slowly on her soft body.

FUN FACTS ● FUN FACTS ● FUN FACTS ● FUN FACTS ● FUN FACTS

Snails leave a trail of slime behind them. The slime makes it easier for them to move.

1. Start with a simple spiral.

2. Draw in a slug-shaped body.

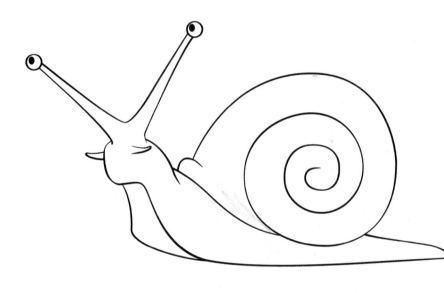

3. Add her feelers and her eyes.

4. Don't forget the slime trail when you colour her in.

Grasshopper

This grasshopper has long back legs that are good for jumping.

He can fly, but not very well.

He has four shorter legs for walking.

He is the same colour as the leaves upon which he lives.

FUN FACTS ● FUN FACTS ● FUN FACTS ● FUN FACTS ● FUN FACTS

Male grasshoppers make music by rubbing their legs against their wings.

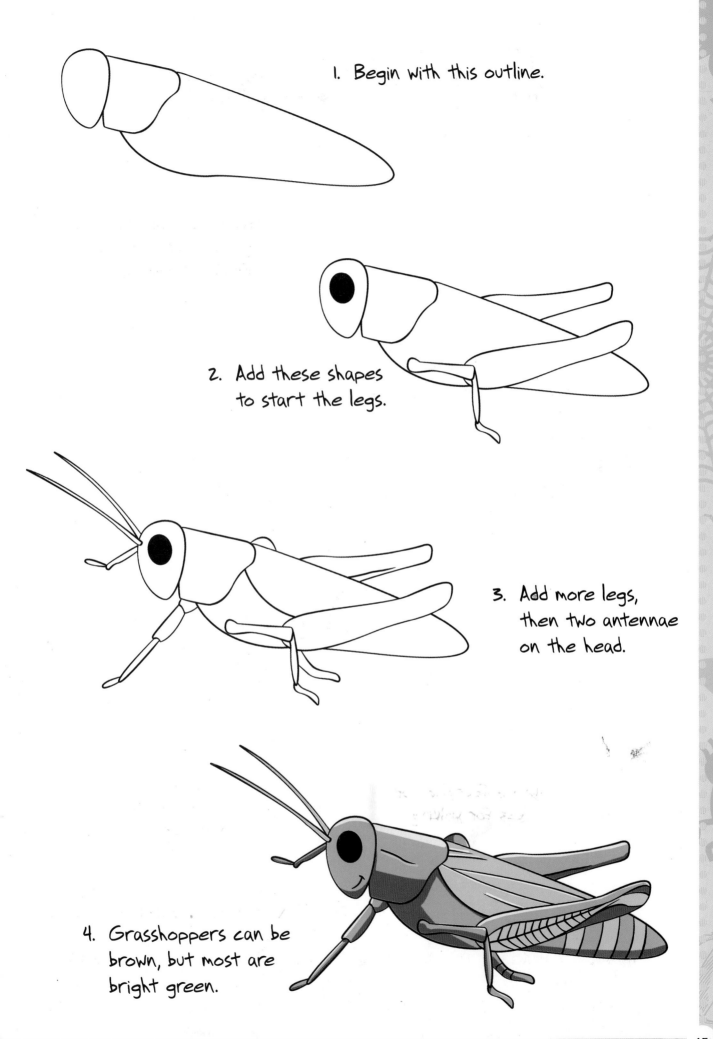

1. Begin with this outline.

2. Add these shapes to start the legs.

3. Add more legs, then two antennae on the head.

4. Grasshoppers can be brown, but most are bright green.

Butterfly

This butterfly is a beautiful blue colour.

Her mouth is like a straw. She drinks nectar from flowers.

She flies in the day, not at night.

She has a long, thin, smooth body.

FUN FACTS ● FUN FACTS ● FUN FACTS ● FUN FACTS ● FUN FACTS

One type of butterfly travels from Canada to Mexico, a journey of over 3,200 km (2,000 miles).

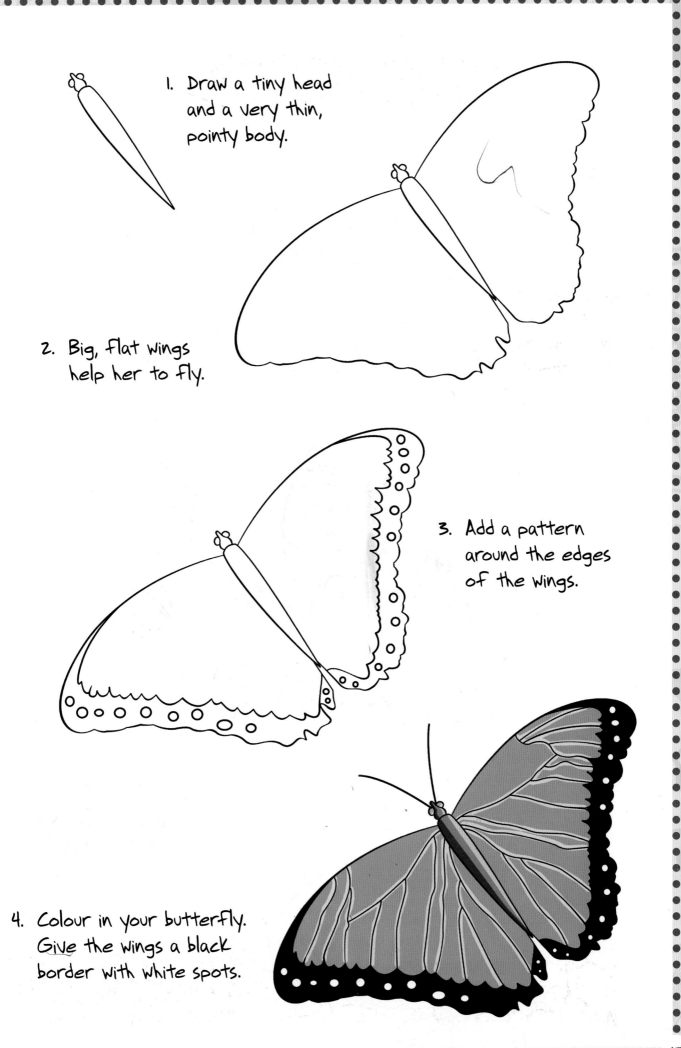

1. Draw a tiny head and a very thin, pointy body.

2. Big, flat wings help her to fly.

3. Add a pattern around the edges of the wings.

4. Colour in your butterfly. Give the wings a black border with white spots.

Ladybird

This ladybird is red with seven black spots.

Her wings are under her hard back.

She eats small, soft insects such as aphids.

She has six legs.

FUN FACTS ● FUN FACTS ● FUN FACTS ● FUN FACTS ● FUN FACTS

In the autumn, ladybirds gather together in a safe, sheltered spot. They sleep through the winter.

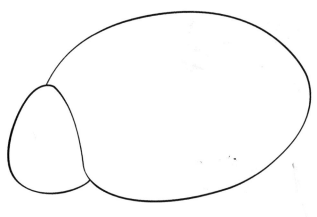

1. Draw two squashed circles for the body and the head.

2. Divide the head and body with simple lines.

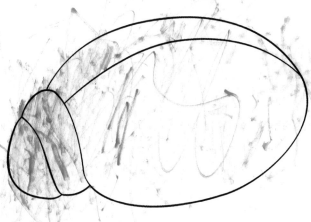

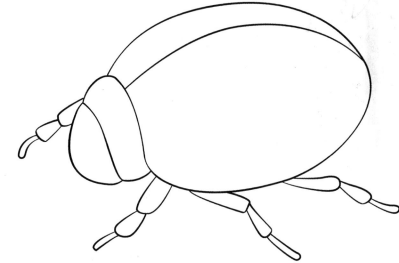

3. Add some short legs. The ladybird has six legs, but you can only see four in this picture.

4. Colour her bright red and add black spots.

Dragonfly

This dragonfly has four wings. She's a very good flier.

She has a brightly coloured body.

She has huge eyes.

She catches her food with her front two legs.

FUN FACTS ● FUN FACTS ● FUN FACTS ● FUN FACTS ● FUN FACTS

Young dragonflies live underwater for several years. Only the adult dragonfly has wings and can fly.

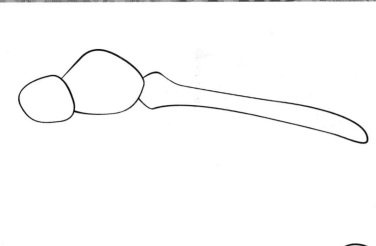

1. Draw these shapes to make the head and body.

2. Add some legs. Dragonflies have six legs, but you can only see four in this picture.

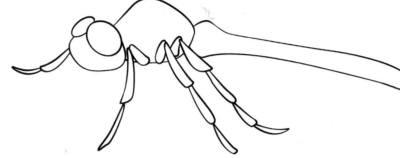

3. Draw four long, narrow wings.

4. Colour the wings pale blue to make them appear see-through.

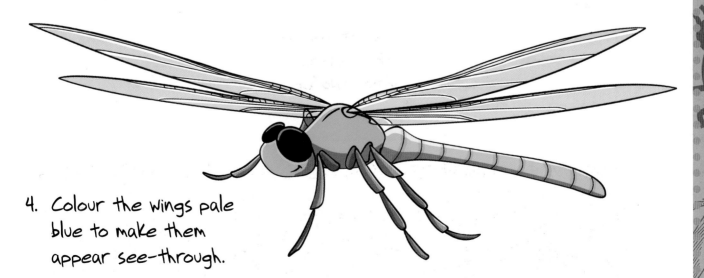

Centipede

She eats insects, spiders and worms. Her bite is poisonous.

Her body is made up of many parts. Each one has two legs.

This centipede has a hard body and lots of legs.

Her back legs are longer than her front ones.

Some centipedes are 25 cm (10 inches) long. They are big enough to eat mice and birds!

1. Draw a long, curvy sausage shape with a circle at the top.

2. Add these lines to show all the parts on her body.

3. Add lots and lots of legs!

4. Don't forget to add the antennae on her head.

Stag beetle

He has big jaws that he uses to fight other males.

This stag beetle has a hard body.

Female stag beetles are smaller than males. They do not have big jaws.

He has wings. They are hidden under here.

FUN FACTS ● FUN FACTS ● FUN FACTS ● FUN FACTS ● FUN FACTS

Stag beetles lay their eggs in old wood. Young beetles live in the wood or under the ground for several years.

1. Two squashed circles and one long oval make the head and body.

2. Add his huge jaws at the front.

3. Draw legs that get thinner at the ends.

4. Finish off by colouring him brown and black.

Moth

This moth has brown wings so that he can hide on trees during the day.

His antennae pick up smells so he can find food or female moths.

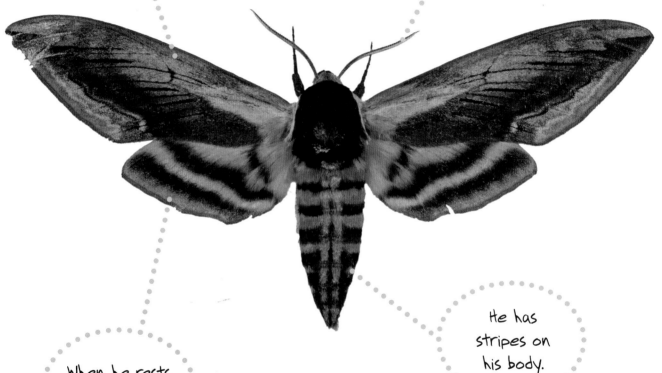

When he rests his wings open flat.

He has stripes on his body.

FUN FACTS ● FUN FACTS ● FUN FACTS ● FUN FACTS ● FUN FACTS

Most moths fly at night. They can get confused by electric lights and fly close to them.

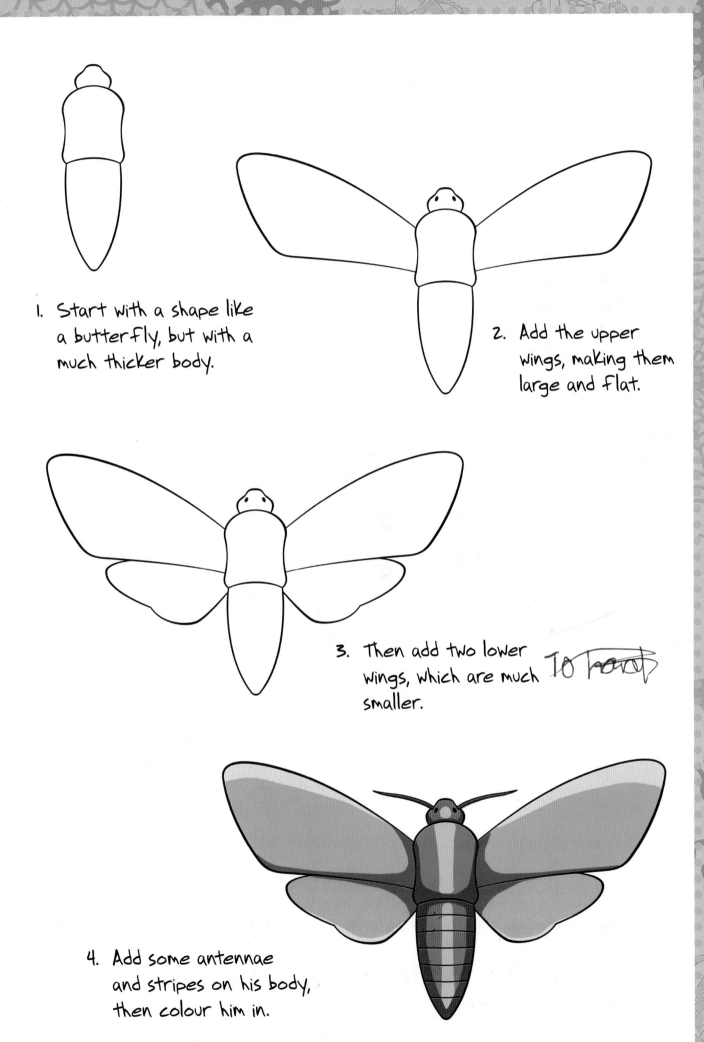

1. Start with a shape like a butterfly, but with a much thicker body.

2. Add the upper wings, making them large and flat.

3. Then add two lower wings, which are much smaller.

4. Add some antennae and stripes on his body, then colour him in.

Ant

This ant has six legs. Her body has four parts.

Ants are small, about 1 cm (half an inch) in length.

Her antennae bend in the middle.

Ants are very strong for their size.

FUN FACTS ● FUN FACTS ● FUN FACTS ● FUN FACTS ● FUN FACTS

Ants live in big groups. Each group has one queen and lots of workers. The workers gather the food and look after the nest.

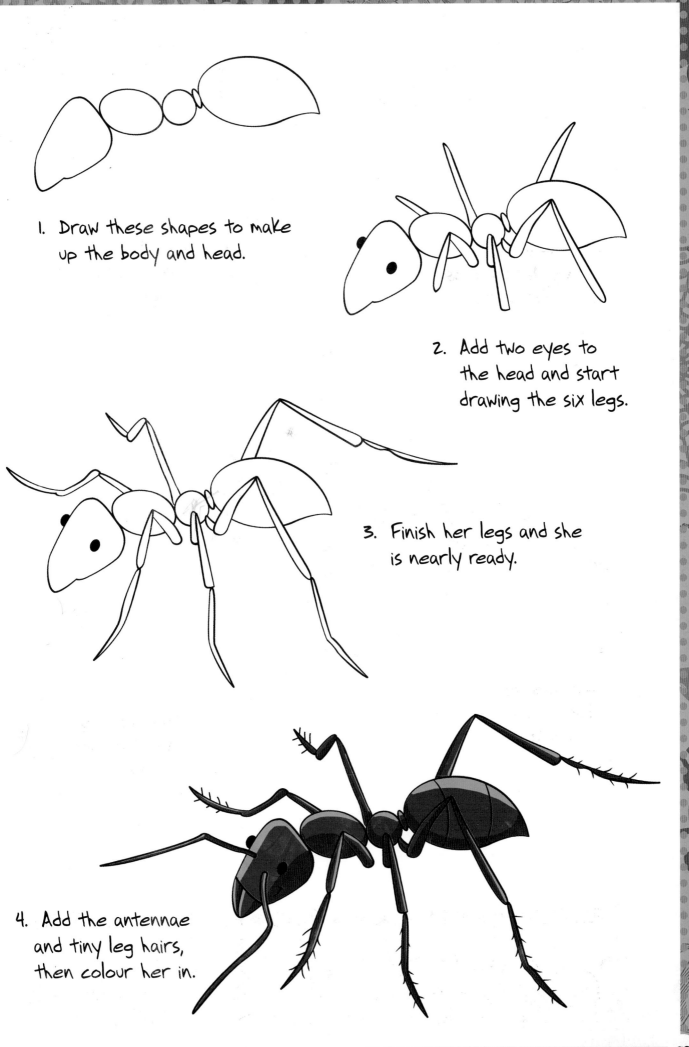

1. Draw these shapes to make up the body and head.

2. Add two eyes to the head and start drawing the six legs.

3. Finish her legs and she is nearly ready.

4. Add the antennae and tiny leg hairs, then colour her in.

Bumblebee

She is brightly coloured, with black and yellow stripes.

She has a sting at the end of her body.

This bumblebee lives with lots of other bees in a nest under the ground.

She is covered in hair to keep her warm.

FUN FACTS ● FUN FACTS ● FUN FACTS ● FUN FACTS ● FUN FACTS

Bees move their wings very fast. Their wings make a buzzing noise when they fly.

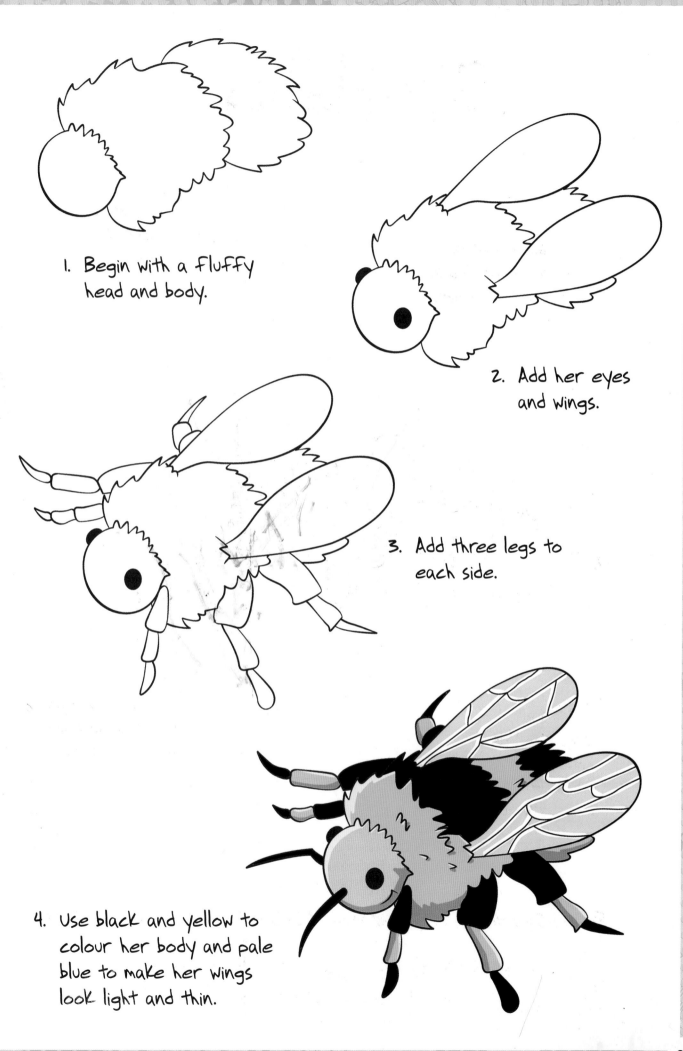

1. Begin with a fluffy head and body.

2. Add her eyes and wings.

3. Add three legs to each side.

4. Use black and yellow to colour her body and pale blue to make her wings look light and thin.

Glossary

antennae the feelers on top of an insect's head, used for smelling and touching

aphid a tiny insect that lives on plants

confused finding something difficult to understand

jaw the outer part of an insect's mouth

journey to travel from one place to another

nectar a sweet liquid made by plants

poisonous contains a liquid that kills or injures an animal

sheltered safe, warm and dry

silk a strong thread made by an insect

slime thick, slippery liquid

sting a sharp point on an animal's body that can be used to hurt another

Further Reading

Bug Drawing Book by Ralph Masiello (Charlesbridge Publishing, 2004)

Insects: Step-by-Step Instructions for 26 Creepy Crawlies by Diana Fisher (Walter Foster, 2007)

Quick Draw Creepy Crawlies by Peter Bull (Kingfisher Books Ltd, 1988)

Websites

BBC Catch and Draw Insects:
http://www.bbc.co.uk/gardening/gardening_with_children/homegrownprojects_bug.shtml

Drawing lessons for children:
www.artistshelpingchildren.org

Natural History Museum: Insects and Spiders:
www.nhm.ac.uk/nature-online/insects

Index

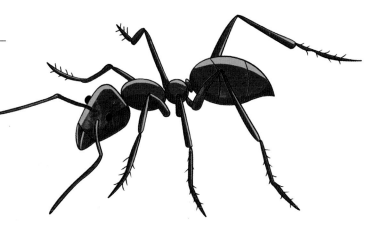